D1361723

SCHOLASTIC
News
Nonfiction Readers®

Let's Talk Riding

by Janice Behrens

Children's Press®
An Imprint of Scholastic Inc.
New York Toronto London Auckland Sydney
Mexico C̶i̶t̶y̶ ... g Kong
D̶e̶...

These content vocabulary word builders are for grades 1–2.

Subject Consultant: Thomas Sawyer, EdD, Professor of Recreation and Sport Management, Indiana State University

Reading Consultant: Cecilia Minden-Cupp, PhD, Reading Specialist and Author, Chapel Hill, North Carolina

Photographs © 2009: Alamy Images: 13 bottom (Jim Allan), 5 top left, 10 right (bilderlounge), 5 bottom left, 10 left (James Sleight), 11 (Homer Sykes); Corbis Images: 2, 21 right (Ron Chapple), 5 top right, 8 left, 9, 23 top right, 23 top left (Kit Houghton), 4 bottom left, 8 (A. Inden/zefa); Digital Railroad/Billy Brown: cover, 5 bottom right, 16; Getty Images: 1, 4 bottom right, 12, 19 (David Handley), 20, 21 left (Bob Langrish), 17 (Mike Powell), 13 top (David Sacks); Peter Arnold Inc.: 15 (Claudius Thiriet/Biosphoto), 23 bottom left (S. Stuewer), 23 bottom right (P. Wegner); PhotoEdit: back cover, 7 (Tom Carter), 4 top, 18 (Michael Newman).

Series Design: Simonsays Design!
Book Production: Scholastic Classroom Magazines

Library of Congress Cataloging-in-Publication Data

Behrens, Janice, 1972–
Let's talk riding / Janice Behrens.
    p. cm.—(Scholastic news nonfiction readers)
Includes bibliographical references and index.
ISBN-13: 978-0-531-13826-7 (lib. bdg.) 978-0-531-20426-9 (pbk.)
ISBN-10: 0-531-13826-7 (lib. bdg.) 0-531-20426-X (pbk.)
1. Horsemanship—Juvenile literature. I. Title.
SF309.2.B44 2008
796—dc22   2007042014

©2009 Scholastic Inc.
All rights reserved. Published in 2009 by Children's Press, an imprint of Scholastic Inc.
Published simultaneously in Canada. Printed in the United States of America.   44
SCHOLASTIC, CHILDREN'S PRESS, and associated logos are trademarks
and/or registered trademarks of Scholastic Inc.
1 2 3 4 5 6 7 8 9 10 R 18 17 16 15 14 13 12 11 10 09

CONTENTS

WORD HUNT

Look for these words as you read. They will be in **bold**.

blue ribbon
(bloo **rib**-uhn)

hooves
(hoovz)

mount
(mount)

bridle
(**brye**-duhl)

groom
(groom)

saddle
(**sad**-uhl)

show jumping
(show **jum**-ping)

Get Ready to Ride!

Some people ride horses as a sport. Some ride just for fun.

Would you like to ride a horse?

Do you want to go for a hack? That's what riders call a horse ride that's just for fun.

Riders take good care of their horses.

One way to care for the horse is to **groom** it. You brush its coat. You make sure its **hooves** are clean. An adult always helps.

groom   **hooves**

A horse should be groomed before each ride. Grooming feels nice to the horse!

After grooming, you can tack up. Tack is what a horse wears.

The **saddle** and **bridle** are part of the tack. A rider sits on the saddle. The bridle helps the rider guide the horse.

bridle

Riders wear special clothes, like helmets and boots.

Now it's time to **mount** up!
That means you get up on
your horse.

All set? Then tell the horse,
"Walk on!"

mount

Moving forward slowly is called a walk.

A fast run is a gallop.

13

After training, a horse knows some words. It knows that *walk on* means go. It knows *whoa* means stop.

Horses have their own way of talking with riders! A horse makes a nicker to say hello.

A nicker sounds like a deep chuckle.

Some riders ride their horses in shows. It takes a lot of training to be in a show. One riding sport is called **show jumping**.

show jumping

In show jumping, the horse leaps over things like fences, walls, and water.

At the show, riders and horses try to win prizes. A **blue ribbon** is first prize.

Win or lose, the best riders show good manners. They are always kind to their horses. That's what riding is all about!

blue ribbon

A horse may nicker when you bring it a treat like a carrot or peppermint.

A HORSE'S BODY

Withers
The top of a horse's shoulders

How tall is your horse?
A horse is measured in hands. One hand is 4 inches (10.16 cm). This horse is about 14 hands high.

Hoof

Rump
The back part of a horse, above its legs

Forelock
The hair on a horse's forehead

Blaze
A white mark on the head of some horses

Tail

Mane

YOUR NEW WORDS

blue ribbon (bloo **rib**-uhn) a kind of prize given for winning a competition

bridle (**brye**-duhl) straps around the horse's head and mouth that help guide the horse

groom (groom) to brush and clean an animal

hooves (hoovz) the feet of horses, deer, and some other animals

mount (mount) to get on or climb up

saddle (**sad**-uhl) a leather seat for a rider on the back of a horse

show jumping (show **jum**-ping) a riding sport in which horses jump over things like fences, walls, and water

FOUR HORSE BREEDS

Morgan

Paint Horse

Palomino

Shetland Pony

INDEX

FIND OUT MORE

Book:

Barnes, Julia. *101 Facts about Horses & Ponies.* Milwaukee: Gareth Stevens, 2002.

Website:

4-H Horse Farm
http://ext.vt.edu/resources/4h/virtualfarm/equine/equine.html

MEET THE AUTHOR

Janice Behrens is a writer and Scholastic editor. She lives in Brooklyn, New York, with her family. Her baby daughter enjoys watching the horses and riders in the park near their home.